AWAKENING SLEEPING BEAUTY:

How Victims of Sexual Abuse Can Reclaim Their Birthright of Wholeness

Janice D. Blackmon

Copyright © 2011 by Janice D. Blackmon

Awakening Sleeping Beauty
How Victims of Domestic Violence and Abuse Can Reclaim Their Birthright of Wholeness
by Janice D. Blackmon

Printed in the United States of America

ISBN 9781619043466

All rights reserved solely by the author. The author guarantees all contents are original and do not infringe upon the legal rights of any other person or work. No part of this book may be reproduced in any form without the permission of the author. The views expressed in this book are not necessarily those of the publisher.

Unless otherwise indicated, Bible quotations are taken from New Living Translation. Copyright © 1984 by Tynsdale House.

TABLE OF CONTENTS

Forward vii
Introduction xi

Chapter One 15
My Story

Chapter Two 26
Their Stories
Cheryl..26
Jackie 29
Pamela 30
Amanda 32
Hanna..34

Chapter Three 37
Methodology

Chapter Four 45
Theoretical Foundation

Chapter Five 68
Statistics on Domestic Violence in the United States

Appendices..71
Bibliography 91

FOREWORD

Writing my Spiritual Autobiography awakened Sleeping Beauty from her long nap. …One morning while in seminary, I awakened desperately to find Sharon Walls. I sat down with my roommate to see if she knew Sharon Walls. I had a message to give her because in a vision, I had seen an obituary of this woman. I could not see the actual face of Sharon Walls. The only thing that I could depict was her face shape and the contour of her hair.

I went on a frantic search for this woman because I felt as though I needed to warn Sharon. No one seemed to know her. This bothered me tremendously because in the past, I had dreams and visions wherein they came to fruition. I felt in my spirit that I should not let this *thing* rest because I wanted to prevent a death or something terrible from happening.

One day I was listening to some inspirational tapes. I heard the minister say, "There comes a time in our lives when we must **share the walls** that we have built." Immediately, a spiritual light bulb came on. Sharon's image flashed before my eyes and I realized that Sharon was no stranger. The contour of her hair was just as I had worn mine in the 70's and 80's during those times of domestic violence and abuse. I was Sharon! The arousal from sleep began.

It was during that time of writing that I realized what the focus of my ministry project should be. I had to dig deeper and deeper within myself to get at the root of the ministry that has been placed there by God. It may not be understood as to why one's roots consist of what it does but there is a responsibility to nurture it so that it may grow into a fruit bearing tree. Initially, the effect of domestic violence issues on congregations was not understood but at the end of my project's implementa- tion, fruit was borne.

The starting point of this fruit bearing process was expected to be dealing with the aftereffects of domestic violence and moving onward towards a healing finish. As a survivor of domestic violence it was not an easy journey since time and space had shielded the issue behind walls of protection. The detours along that journey were not only surprising to the members of the focus group; it was surprising to me.

The first surprise came when the topic of domestic violence emerged in various conversations throughout the congregation and beyond. It was overwhelming how much domestic violence was prevalent at the church where I served as pastor. It was also alarming and comforting for me to know that there are organizations and indi- viduals who are ready to speak out against the crime of domestic violence. It was amazing to me because I was not aware of the various programs and agencies that exist that are advocates for the cause of domestic violence. On the other hand there are still not enough agencies and churches with their doors open for this cause.

Relatives and friends of victims informed me of their knowledge of their loved ones' abuse. Victims and survivors began to come out of the woodwork which made it easy to select those who would be a part of the ministry model. Since min- istries are created out of a need, the participant's stories helped to shape the project.

It is startling for pastors to serve congregations and not realize who it is they are serving. In a situation such as domestic violence the alarm however is not that surprising.

Although there have been great leaps in addressing domestic violence a degree of secrecy still looms over the issue. It was that air of secrecy that caused me to wonder, how much of their stories would the group members share? How much of my story should be told, after all I was their pastor. These questions were answered the moment the first woman arrived for the one-on-one interview. The first client, as with the other four partici- pants came in ready to tell her story.

INTRODUCTION

Domestic violence is defined by the Michigan Domestic Violence Prevention and Treatment Board as "the occurrence of any of the following acts by a person that is not an act of self-defense; causing or attempting to cause physical or mental harm to a family or household member; placing a family or household member in fear of physical or mental harm; causing or attempting to cause a family or household member to engage in involuntary sexual activity by force, threat of force, or duress; and/or engaging in activity toward a family or household member that would cause a reasonable person to feel terrorized, frightened, intimidated, threatened, harassed, or molested."[1]

Rarely does the violence noticeably show up in the beginning of a relationship but it starts out gradually and then escalates. It can occur in any combination and can last for years. Women involved in heterosexual relationships are usually the victims of domestic violence. Men involved in heterosexual relationships can also be victims. Domestic violence does occur in same sex relationships. Domestic

---

[1] Department of Human Services, *Michigan Resource Center on Domestic and Sexual Violence*, *MDVPTB's Definition of Domestic Violence*. From http://www.michigan.gov/dhs/0,1607-124-5460_7261-15005—,00.html. Accessed May 22, 2007.

violence is not limited to a particular culture, race, religion or socio-economic class. There is no excuse for domestic violence behavior. It is learned and reinforced:

- through observation
- through experience
- in culture and in society
- in the family
- in communities including schools and peer groups
- in faith, religious, and spiritual institutions
- through our failure to hold batterers accountable for their actions[2]

Domestic violence and abuse is being accepted by some teenagers. One out of 10 high school students will experience physical violence from someone they are dating.[3] Teens often confuse jealousy with love. They lack experience and perspec- tive regarding what a healthy dating relationship can be. Because of their striving for independence, teenagers tend to not want to seek advice from counselors or clergy. When advice is given, the teenager should be reassured that their situation will be handled discreetly.

The aftereffects of domestic violence are long lasting. Unfortunately, the bruises of the psychological abuse last longer than those of the physical. After leaving the relationship, there are some symptoms which the survivors exemplify and must be addressed. Symptoms include but are not limited to the following:

- Heart palpitations or breaking into a cold sweat when you see violence on TV

---

[2] Ibid., 10.

[3] American Psychological Association, *"Love shouldn't hurt: Teens"* http://www.apa.org/pi/cyf/teen.pdf.. (Accessed October 10, 2007).

- Waking up in a state of panic from dreams of being chased by your abuser
- Cleansing obsessively to avoid thinking about the abuse
- Not answering the phone because you think it might be your abuser
- Not taking pleasure in activities you used to enjoy
- Not feeling close to anyone
- Not being able to walk down the street without looking around and worrying that you will run into your abuser
- Not being able to get more than four or five hours of sleep, and not restful sleep at that
- Trying to read and finding yourself stuck on the same page for twenty minutes
- Yelling at the kids for little things
- Felling guilty that the children witnessed the abuse or are being deprived of their father
- Feeling guilty about not having been able to get your partner to change
- Feeling guilty about not having broken off the relationship sooner[4]

Chapter One is entitled, My Story. It is a synopsis of my personal story. This chapter includes a portion of the spiritual autobiography of my experiences of domestic violence and abuse. Chapter Two gives a brief account of the experiences of five women who shared their stories. These women were prayerfully chosen to participate in the ministry project. Their names are not real however, their stories are very real. Chapter Three gives the methodology of the project. It

---

[4] Edward S. Kubany, Mari A. McCaig, and Janet R. Laconsay, *Healing the Trauma of Domestic Violence, A Workbook for Women* (Oakland, CA: New Harbinger Publications, Inc., 2004), 1-2.

also explains what happened when the project was implemented and describes how the data was collected. Chapter Four is a biblical, theological, and historical perspective of domestic violence. Chapter Five consists of some alarming statistics of abuse in the United States with an emphasis on the state of Michigan. The Appendices include the forms, litanies, tools and session outlines used during the ministry project. This information may be helpful in establishing or enhancing your ministry. The Bibliography contains reference books, CD's, websites and recordings used throughout the project and the writing of this book.

CHAPTER ONE

MY STORY

I am a survivor of 13 years of domestic violence. I was born to Christian parents and grew up in a non-violent home. They instilled good morals and values into my life. Both parents were musicians and the gift of musicianship was passed on to me. In 1974, I was awarded a music scholarship to Alcorn State University in Lorman, Mississippi where I majored in voice.

I left Alcorn State University as a sophomore on the dean's list. On December 23, 1975, at the age of 19, I married my high school sweetheart, who was an Army Private, First Class. Shortly thereafter we moved to Fort Benning, Georgia. In February 1976, the marital bliss ended on the day that we prepared to go to a friend's birthday party. It was on this occasion that I received the first sign of physical abuse by my husband in the form of numerous slaps to my face.

Slipping away from God and needing to feel God's presence, I knelt at the side of my bed to pray. My husband told me to get up off of my knees and so I did; from then on I prayed alone, if at all.

I thought that if I joined in the myriad of parities with my husband and his friends, maybe the violence and abuse would stop. From 1976-1984, I stayed away from God even though there was still a part of me that longed for God.

In 1977, my husband was assigned a tour of duty in South Korea. I joined him in Korea as a non-government sponsored spouse. This meant that we were respon- sible for travel and residential housing. The music was still in my bones. During the end of this tour of duty in 1978, I visited the Army chapel and played the piano, when I thought that no one was listening but God. The Army Chaplin heard me and approached me about playing for the upcoming revival. Although he offered to change the revival date so that I could provide music my husband said, "No!"

My husband was assigned to Fort Hood, Texas from 1978-1982. After years of marriage and no children, I decided in 1979 to have an infertility work-up. The first appointment had to be cancelled because the night before, he attacked. I had some old luggage, the kind that was very hard that was opened on the bed. He picked me up and threw me on the bed onto the luggage. My thigh was so badly bruised that I knew if I kept the appointment I would have to give some kind of explanation as to what happened.

After major surgery, doctors told us that they had done all they could. If no con- ception took place within six months to a year, there was nothing else to be done.

During this period of time, my father's gospel singing group, in Alabama, recorded an album and sent it to me in Texas. My husband would wait until we were partying to play the album. As a result, I would have to listen to "Take Time Out for Jesus" and "Look to Jesus" while the party was in full swing. My husband knew that it aggravated me when he did that. He also knew that my father and I were close. From time to time my husband would make offensive and threatening com- ments about my family. For years, life was "a walk on pins and needles" for me.

My husband was re-assigned to South Korea for a second tour of duty. I accom- panied him and this time the tour was government sponsored. During this time, the physical and mental abuse heightened during the years from 1982-1984. Once, my husband was due to have guard duty, for the next day and a half. The night before he was to serve he was not home and so I went to the club where I knew he was. When he saw me he was so upset. He made me sit down at a table and he sat across from me with his hand on a bottle. He threatened to hit me with it if I said anything or moved from the table. I managed to leave the club and went on compound (the army base) to talk with a female soldier. Unfortunately for me she was not in. My husband followed me and I tripped and fell to the ground. While on the ground he kicked me and told me to get up. I tried fixing my clothes and hair because we had to walk through the guarded gate. The military police asked was I alright and I said, "Yes," because I did not want to get my husband in trouble. When we returned to the place we were living, he apologized for what he had done. By that time I had a swollen lip and a black eye.

I was employed as the receptionist for the Army Education Center in Taegu, Korea at Camp Walker which allowed me to meet a lot of people. I got involved in the community activities. While in Korea, and my husband was away, the American Theater Group held auditions for, *The Sound of Music*. I tried out and received the acting role of Mother Abyss. I was offered the lead but turned it down because I knew that my husband was not going to let me kiss another man, especially a white man. I was awarded best supporting actress for my role as the nun. I felt that once again the hills in my life were alive with the *sound of music*. Although my husband attended one of the productions he failed to exhibit any signs of expression of approval or disapproval.

Awakening Sleeping Beauty

At the Army Education Center, I befriended a female co-worker who was Korean. Her father was an Evangelical pastor and she invited me to her church to sing hymns. It did not matter that I could not speak Korean. When I sang, *Amazing Grace*, the expression on the faces of those within the congregation let me know that they understood what I was singing. God's grace kept me holding on to my faith in spite of the domestic violence.

Upon finding out that I was pregnant with our first child, in 1984 that did not stop the physical and mental abuse. The parties stopped for me, however. In the spring of 1984, the Army sent us back to Fort Hood, Texas. The mental abuse con- tinued and he constantly accused me of having an affair. He even insinuated that the baby born October 10, 1984, was not his. He began staying away from home on a regular basis. That brought some relief and anxiety for me.

Fourteen months later, our second child was born on Christmas Day 1985. My husband said, "If you get pregnant again, it would be without me." In January 1986, my husband was generally discharged from the Army because of his drug abuse. In 1986, we all returned to Birmingham, Alabama. His cocaine habit and "the other woman" took him away from the house days at a time. However, the domestic vio- lence continued whenever he returned home.

Up until this time, I failed to seek help or assistance from anyone. Even though I had wandered away from God, I knew that a life time of domestic violence and abuse was not the plan for my life or the lives of my children. I was employed by AmSouth Bank. I took on a second job at Blue Cross and Blue Shield of Alabama. I started going back to church and began realizing that God had something better for us.

As the abuse continued, I began calling 911 for help. The police would come to the house but we would act as if everything was alright. On one of the calls, my husband was taken to jail because the police observed that some kind of altercation had taken place in the house. I had him released from jail and did not press charges. Today, victims may not drop charges without the consent of the prosecutor's office and it is not that easy to be released because of the strict laws against perpetrators of domestic violence.

Since I really wanted to save the marriage for the children's sake, I began going with my husband to the Veterans Administration Hospital to receive counseling for his drug abuse. Because of the counselor's insight he asked me to return for counseling without my husband. Somehow the counselor knew that more than drug abuse was the problem. When I returned and spoke with him, I shared my plight of physical and emotional abuse by my husband. He advised me to get out of the relationship before I would be killed. Consequently, in 1989, my husband and I divorced.

In April, 1990, my father died. It was during that same year that I and my mother became musicians for a small Baptist church. I played the piano and my mother played the organ.

The divorce and the death of my father left an ominous void in my life. In November, 1990, I remarried my husband. This time there was no violence but I started noticing old tendencies. The atmosphere was tensed as if a storm was brewing. My husband began staying out overnight. One day while my husband was out, I packed my 1984 Maxima and loaded everything I could in the trunk and drove off. He did not know that we were gone until the evening of the following day. Six months into my second marriage to him I divorced him for the last time.

A pattern of unhealthy relationships set in. Only two years later I met and mar- ried an unemployed younger man in February, 1992. During this time I had to have surgery. Having used all of my sick time and vacation from Blue Cross and Blue Shield, there was no income for six weeks. It was not a fighting relationship but it was a mentally abusive relationship. I discovered that my new husband had a past life of gangs, rape, and drugs. Soon afterwards he was arrested. I divorced him after six months of marriage because of his sordid life. Because of his past conduct, the judge gladly allowed me to change my last name back to Blackmon so that my children and I could have the same name.

Although my mother tried to financially support me and the children, it became impossible for this to continue to happen. My mother said, "Baby, come on home." In August, 1992, I and my children moved in with my mother. Mama nurtured me through prayer and words of encouragement. My relationship with God is what held me together during that time period of 1976-1992. Our relationship became stronger as I sought God for direction for the lives of both me and my children.

The Call to Ministry

During the years of 1992-1994, I wrote Gospel music and had two selections presented at the Gospel Music Workshop of America as new children's music: *Josiah* and *He Just Might Be Your Angel*. Josiah was a young righteous King of Israel. Upon reading the Book of the Law he realized that his righteousness was not good enough. This prompted me to ask, "How can God use me knowing that I am not perfect?" I pondered that question in my heart.

One night in a vision I saw the moon in the sky and a circle of people. I was included in that circle but where I stood indented it, making it imperfect. I felt in my spirit the song, *Will the Circle be Unbroken*. The moon fell to the earth and burst into bright red blood. When I awakened I was about to become frightened. Before fear over whelmed me, the Holy Spirit said, "There is only one perfect person who waked this earth and His name is Jesus. The only thing you need to do is keep pressing toward the mark." Feeling special I wrote the song, *The Visitor*. The lyrics are as follows:

> The Holy Spirit visits me and sets my captive soul free.
> So often time He comes just when I'm not thinking of Him at all.
> But when He comes I surely know it was He, He calls to my remembrance. So glad to know He cares for me and takes the time to comfort me.
>
> From time to time I have a thought that lingers on my mind for days. The Holy Spirit says to me, my child lean not to your own ways. Sometimes when I am fast asleep, He sweetly, gently speaks to me. So glad to know he cares for me and takes the time to comfort me.
>
> Wasn't that so nice of Him to leave a friend that would defend. The Comforter was given so that we don't have to be alone.
> A gift, a gift from God above to keep us safe from hurt and harm,
> The Visitor, my Comforter, he cares for me, so glad to know He cares for me,
> So glad to know he cares for me, and takes the time to comfort me.[5]

I wrote another song entitled, He Just Might Be Your Angel. It was inspired by the homeless situation in the city. It grieved my heart to pass by them on the way to church. Hebrews 13:2 says to be carful to entertain strangers. Below are some of the lyrics.

---

[5] Janice D. Blackmon, *The Visitor* (Birmingham, AL: Professionals for Christ Ministries and Publications, 1993).

Don't walk away and turn up your nose when a wino asks you for dime.
Do you turn your head when the homeless ask for bread? Then you pretend he's not even there.
Be careful, beware for he just might be your angel. There are those who have entertained them unaware.[6]

During the same time period, I had a mystical experience as I passed the piano at 3:13 A.M. I heard a voice. Everyone was asleep. I could not make out what was said but I was not frightened. The presence of the voice was one of peace and intel- ligence. I believe that God was letting me know that there was more for me to do than write music.

A monetary award was given to me by the Gospel Music Workshop of America. I used it for a deposit on an apartment. My dreams and visions continued. One night I was praying in the bedroom and continued praying as I walked to the living room. I asked God, "What do you want from me?" After all, I was a musician and lyricist. On the night of October 25, 1994, God told me to preach the word.

Not long after accepting the call to preach, I asked the Lord to go deep inside of me and pull out anything that would cause a hindrance to my ministry. The Holy Spirit said, "Don't base your life on what you perceive others think of you." For so many years I had been called everything but a child of God. I had to begin seeing myself as God sees me.

My mother and I continued serving as musicians for the small Baptist church. Each time I had an experience, I would share it with the pastor of the church. After receiving the call to preach I approached the pastor and he did not seem surprised.

---

[6] Janice D. Blackmon, *He Just Might Be Your Angel* (Birmingham, AL: Professionals for Christ Ministries and Publications, 1994).

He had a meeting with his Deacon Board. Later, he told me that I would not be preaching at the church. I knew nothing else but to continue playing the piano.

The Holy Spirit said, "I'm going to send you somewhere that you can better serve." Shortly thereafter, a co-worker of mine told me that her church, Southside Christian Methodist Episcopal Church was looking for musician. I wanted to leave the Baptist church in the right spirit. I prayed to God as to how to leave it. I was directed to I Corinthians 2:9 which says, "But it is written, Eye hath not seen, nor ear heard, neither have entered into the heart of man, the things which God hath prepared for them that love him." I placed this in a letter to be read to the church. It was given to the chairman of the Deacon Board to be read to the congregation. He acted as if he was reading the letter but made up his own explanation.

I left the Baptist church and became the musician for Southside C.M.E. Church in Birmingham, Alabama. When I shared with the pastor, Rev. Dr. Sylvester Williams, about my call to preach the gospel he said, "We must get you off of the piano into the pulpit." I preached my first sermon on March 26, 1995 and received my license April 1, 1995. I was ordained Deacon and Elder in 1997 and assigned as pastor of the Smith Chapel C.M.E. Church in August, 1997.

I met ministers who were second, third, and fourth generation preachers. I felt like the prophet Amos who did not come from a line of prophets. I was minding my own business and did not come from a family of preachers.

My great-grand mother, Gertrude, was in her 90's at this time. She shared with me about Ella Christian-Martin, who was Gertrude's grand mother. Ella was a mid- wife and preacher in the late 1800's and the turn of the century. It was said that she would stand in the roads of Columbiana, Alabama, declaring God's word. The people in the city did not appreciate her actions and wanted to get rid of her. They decided not to because they had no one else who "catch the babies." This knowl- edge gave me a sense of peace and belonging among my peers.

To further understand the C.M.E. church, I enrolled in the Phillips School of Theology at the Interdenominational Theological Center in Atlanta, Georgia. One morning while in seminary, I awakened desperately to find Sharon Walls. I sat down with my roommate to see if she knew Sharon Walls. I had a message to give her because in a vision, I had seen an obituary of this woman. I could not see the actual face of Sharon Walls. The only thing that I could depict was her face shape and the contour of her hair.

I went on a frantic search for this woman because I felt as though I needed to warn Sharon. No one seemed to know her. This bothered me tremendously because in the past, I had dreams and visions wherein they came to fruition. I felt in my spirit that I should not let this *thing* rest because I wanted to prevent a death or something terrible from happening.

One day I was listening to some inspirational tapes. I heard the minister say, "There comes a time in our lives when we must **share the walls** that we have built." Immediately, a spiritual light bulb came on. Sharon's image flashed before my eyes and I realized that Sharon was no stranger. The contour of her hair was just as I had worn mine in the 70's and 80's during those times of domestic violence and abuse. I was Sharon!

As the Holy Spirit dealt with me, I realized that it was during that period that I had built up walls to protect myself against hurt, fear, and rejection. In order for me to be free to serve as God wanted me to, I had to **share the walls**. I needed to talk about and deal with the unresolved issues in my life. I had learned to suppress my feeling by hiding them behind walls, which could not be penetrated.

In their book, *Boundaries*, Dr. Henry Cloud and Dr. John Townsend state, "Boundaries are suppose to be able to 'breathe,' to be like fences with a gate that can let the good in and the bad out. Individuals with walls for boundaries can let in neither bad nor good. No one touches them."[7] I believe that if people do not share their domestic violence experiences, they will build walls which will be hard to penetrate.

In *Healing the Trauma of Domestic Violence: A workbook for Women*, the authors reveal, "A survivor may suffer aftereffects of having been physically and mentally abused."[8] Abnormal behavior may manifest when a survivor of domestic violence does not adequately deal with her experience. She is therefore left alone with trying to understand what happened to her. It is my belief that more ministries need to be created that will give survivors of domestic violence a platform on which they can share their experiences. In the following chapter, you will hear from some survivors. Hear their stories.

---

[7] Henry Cloud and John Townsend, *Boundaries* (Grand Rapids, MI: Zondervan, 1992), 52.

[8] Edward S. Kubany, Mari A. McCaig, and Janet R. Laconsay, *Healing the Trauma of Domestic Violence; A Workbook for Women* (Oakland, CA: New Harbinger Publications, Inc. 2004), 1.

CHAPTER TWO

THEIR STORIES

In recent years many incidents of domestic violence have made the news. It was therefore not too hard to hear discussions about it within the church. The behavior of some women was noticed during these conversations. Some of the women were adamantly against domestic violence when some others were indif- ferent. On one occasion a woman commented that domestic violence was a private affair between the parties involved. Ironically she is one of the participants of the group. Fictitious names have been given to the women.

Cheryl's Story

Cheryl is a 44 year old mother of two teenagers, a boy and a girl. She was very open and nervously started talking the moment she came into my home. She referred to her abuser as a "sperm donor" that was on crack. She said, "Emotional wounds are the deepest," even though she still carries a bullet in her left buttocks. Her abuse started when she was 27 years old, prior to her becoming pregnant with her son a year later. Being pregnant did not stop the abuse.

As she was sharing she began remembering things that she had not thought about for a long time.

One of the traits of those who are dealing with the after-effects of domestic vio- lence is the ability to forget things they do not want to remember. She shared that she had an appointment at the clinic but she never made it to the doctor's office, where she was employed. Her abuser thought that she was planning to meet the man who gave her a glance as she was getting ready to go in. She was threatened to be beaten and left alone. Cheryl never knew when her abuser was going to attack. Life for a victim of domestic violence is the feeling of walking on egg shells because the victim tries to keep the abuser from attacking.

During the course of her interview, Cheryl referred to herself as being or acting stupid five different times. I wondered if this is one of the adjectives that her abuser used to describe her. The victim of a domestic violence situation is usually called out of their name over and over again until it is internalized. This is why self esteem has to be restored.

After a beating at the abuser's parent's home, the client took refuge in the home of her biological father who lived in another state. She soon returned to Michigan and moved in with her abuser. This is a pattern among victims; they return to what they are accustomed. Cheryl remembers keeping a sledge hammer underneath their bed and thought about using it on her abuser but she was too afraid.

Cheryl shared many incidents but the following account was most shocking to me. She and her abuser had gone to the home of a friend of his. This home was nothing more than a shack. Cheryl could not determine whether the friend was male or female. Everybody in the house, with the exception of the Cheryl, was taking drugs. Her abuser had recently bought a gun and had in with him. He kept taunting her about having an ATM card that she did not tell him about. Accusations were being hurled at her. He then shot her in the left knee but the bullet exited. The abuser proceeded to shoot her two more times in the knees. Each time he would turn the music up loud. The song that was playing was "Trust in God, Always." This was a song that she used to sing as a duet with her sister.

All the wile this is taking place, the abuser kept asking the Cheryl, "What do you want to get the kids to wear?" He then asked her, "What do you want to wear?" She realized later that he was referring to the attire for her funeral. They stayed at the house all night long until her abuser said he was tired, wanted to get the kids who were at her mother's house, and go home.

The client was afraid to go to the police. When they got home the abuser ran bath water for her and asked, "Why did you make me do this to you?" She poured Epsom salt into the water as her daughter asked, "What happened to you?" Cheryl told her seven year old daughter that her daddy had shot her. I could only imagine what went through the mind of that little girl and how it affected her. There is a trend that if a child is in an abusive home, they will either become the abuser or the abused.

It was not until sometime later that Cheryl's eyes were opened. Her abuser started using the children to humiliate her. When her children came home from school, the abuser would have the call their mother on her job and say, "Hey Bitch, I'm home." This would be repeated several times with the abuser then coming on the line.

Cheryl finally told her mother that she had been shot several times. With the help of a family friend the Cheryl eluded her abuser and went to the police station. The police said that the wounds were too old. However she had a wound from the night before where the abuser had broken a glass on her leg. The officers asked her, "What was her abuser's name?" When he gave them his name they became very interested because there was a warrant out for his arrest. She gave them his location but she feared because the children were with him. When the officers entered the house, the abuser attempted to pick up their son but the officers were able to subdue him. He said he was merely picking up his son to give him a hug. He was taken to jail in October 1999. While he was incarcerated, Cheryl received permission to marry him. The marriage was never consummated because the client divorced him upon his release in 2004.

Cheryl only communicates with her ex-husband in reference to the children. Her son expresses that he wants his father in his life. Her daughter has no respect for her father and has threatened him that if he tries to hurt her mother again, some- body is going to die.

Jackie's Story

Jackie is a 56 year old mother of three adult children, one son and two daugh- ters. Her husband mentally abused her from the age of nineteen up until the time he had a stroke in 1996. The stroke not only affected his physical ability but it totally altered his personality, whereas he is more subdued and kind.

Jackie experienced domestic violence as a teenager at the age of 16. Her first abuser is now deceased and not the father of her children. He was homeless and she would allow him to sleep in their basement. When her mother found out, she permitted him to continue to sleep there. Jackie and her boyfriend would have sex in vacant apartment buildings. The abuse would happen during sex.

She kept a diary of her experiences and her youngest brother found it and showed it to their mother. Jackie's mother kept a close eye on her by taking her to the daily bingo games. Therefore when the client's boyfriend came around, she was nowhere to be found. He moved on and she met and married her husband at age nineteen.

The mental abuse began immediately. It is a tendency for victims of domestic violence to enter into another abusive relationship until the pattern is broken. Jackie explained how her husband controlled and accused her of having affairs. He also used to the children against her by not feeding the when she was at work nor changed their diapers. He would not let her visit with her family with the children. Jackie says that she has experienced two nervous breakdowns since the marriage.

When Jackie entered my home, her conversation was immediately about her children. During the time of my research, one daughter was currently in an abusive relationship. I found that the Jackie's attitude toward her daughter was perplexing. The client expressed that she does not want to hear about her daughter's domestic violence situation anymore. When asked why, the client was rather adamant. The client feels that because she has talked with her daughter and so have I, that the daughter should leave her abuser. I agreed with her about the leaving but I also think that the client should be more understanding about the situation.

The other daughter is a lesbian who was in a domestic violence relationship with another woman. She has since left that relationship. This is evidence that domestic violence can go from generation to generation.

Jackie's husband comes from a violent home. She says that her husband's father had eleven children by his wife and six by his wife's sister. The extent of the vio- lence will be discussed by Pamela who is the niece of Jackie's husband.

Pamela's Story

Pamela is the youngest of the women studied. She is 39 years old with a teenage son and daughter by her abuser. She was eighteen when she moved in with her abuser and that is when the physical and mental abuse began. Fights happened when her boyfriend would get drunk. She left the relationship in 2005.

Pamela did not want to tell her family because she says she was in denial and wanted to protect him. She told her mother and other family members also knew of the abuse. Her boyfriend would apologize and promise not to do it again. The situ- ation waned but soon afterwards the abuse would start again.

Pamela informed me that her mother was abused by boyfriends that she would bring to the house. The children heard the fights even though they pretended to be asleep. The client says that she thinks it is a "generational curse." Many of her mother's brothers and sisters experienced abuse.

I asked her, "What relationship is Jackie to you?" She said that Jackie's hus- band is her mother's uncle, her grandfather's son. She said that her uncle was also abused. Pamela says that her abuser's mother was abused by his father and the client's boyfriend was a witness. The client also says that all of her boyfriend's siblings are abusers. The boyfriend was also abused by his biology teacher. Again, I can not help but to conclude that abuse begat abuse.

Pamela's children also witnessed the abuse of her boyfriend toward her. He son was eight or nine years old while her daughter was either three or four years old. She says that her children had been affected by the abuse. She says that her son, who was 21 years old during the time of the project, says that he will never be like his daddy and that he will be a gentleman. Her son is protective of her; he intervened between his mother and father. She says that both of her children were nervous during the time of the abuse.

Pamela relies on her strong faith in God even though she has since then been in another controlling relationship of which she ended. Just like Cheryl, she feels that if she had stayed with her children's father, someone would have been killed because they both had guns. At the time of the interview, she expresses guilt for having stayed in the relationship for so long.

Amanda's Story

Amanda is a 58 year old mother of two daughters. I had to go to her home to get the personal interview because of medical reasons. It was a little uncomfortable for everybody because her eleven year old granddaughter was there. Amanda spoke rather quietly, however I was able to get the interview. Her daughter came to pick up her child and the interview went more smoothly.

Amanda shared that when she was between 45 and 48 years old, a scene flashed before her eyes. The scene was that of her uncle, her mother's brother, getting off of her. After leaving work one day she went to the street where her family lived when she was seven years old. She drove by the house and she knew that something had happened there.

Later that evening she called her oldest brother to ask him if he remembers any- thing about her and their uncle. Her brother says he remembers the uncle coming out of her room a couple of times when they were children but he did not know what happened inside. The youngest brother also heard the discussion and sug- gested that they tell their parents who were out working in the yard.

When the Amanda's mother was asked about the situation she said nothing had happened. But the following day her mother called and said she knew that some- thing had happened. Amanda reassured her mother that she was not planning to do anything to the uncle she just wanted to know the truth.

Amanda shared that she and her mother has never been on good terms. She said that her mother had a still born child before she was born. Her mother was always hard on her and did not encourage her. The mother often talked bout the

Amanda's appearance and constantly told her that she would never be anything in life. Amanda is obese but is taking the proper steps to lose weight.

She shared her experience with her pastor who advised her to visit her uncle. He was in the nursing home when she went to see him. He is paralyzed from the waist down. He was an alcoholic and has suffered a brain hemorrhage. When she saw the condition that he was in and the fact that his mind was not all there, she did not say anything to him about the abuse. She said that she knew in her spirit that she had forgiven him but she expressed that she never liked him. Her uncle is still in the nursing home and she does not go by often to see him.

Amanda's first husband was a physical abuser who came from a violent home. When her father found out about the abuse, he went after him. Amanda begged her father not to kill her husband. Her father gave her a switch blade to carry so that "anything black and ashy that came toward her had better look out." The marriage ended after six months. Her first husband was murdered.

Amanda married her second husband twice. He is the father of her children. She said that the relationship was going well until she found out that he was a homo- sexual. He did not physically abuse her but he verbally abused her. At this point I wondered how the relationship could be going well when he was verbally abusing her. He later became a minister but there was some controversy about him and a member of the choir.

From that point on the client had several more relationships, notably with leaders in the church. Her last relationship was with the brother of an elder in the church. The brother was newly released from jail and the elder thought that the client would be somebody good for him. He verbally abused her by talking about her figure and using her financially. He went back to jail and the client has since cut off communication with him.

Amanda is not in a relationship right now, even though she hopes to be someday. She says that she is waiting on God to send her someone. The unfortunate thing about this situation is that Amanda's youngest daughter is in an abusive relation- ship. She shared this with me after the project was complete. Amanda has offered her home to her daughter as a place of refuge.

Hanna's Story

Hanna is not the original person selected for the project; however there is pur- pose in everything. She is a 45 year old mother of five from St. Croix, Virgin Islands. Even though she gave the personal interview, she did not come back to participate in the focus group. That is most unfortunate because I believe that she could have possibly benefited from the group participation.

Hanna's marriage to her abuser is her second marriage. Her first marriage ended because of infidelity on her husband's part. Out of all of the other participants, Hanna and her second husband are the only ones who received formal counseling as a couple. They went for four months. This was to no avail because the husband had an ulterior motive for marrying her; he needed a permanent green card because he was from the Dominican Republic. When he got the ten year card, he began physically abusing the client. His getting the card took a succession of marriages. Unknowingly, the Hanna was wife number five. They were married for eight years.

All of her children were born at the time of the abuse. Her husband is the father of her last two children. She tried not to provoke him or fight with him so she would walk away. Her ignoring him made him angrier and he would punch her in the back and catch her by the hair. He would leave the house and stay out all night. When he returned in the morning, he would tear off her night clothes and push his fingers into her vagina to see if she had been with another man. She did not share this with anyone; not even her older children who were there in the house.

The younger children, a son and daughter were aware of the abuse. The son slept in the same bedroom. At age three, he would say to the father, "Papito stop." But the father would tell him to shut up and go to sleep.

When they went to court to settle the green card issue, she discovered that he had a criminal record. The client explained to the court what had been going on, but since the laws were not as they are now, the officers told her that she had to go back home because he was her husband. The house they lived in belonged to the client and she felt that she and her children had nowhere else to go; her husband should have left but he did not.

The violence escalated until she was admitted into the hospital. He was arrested and sentenced. The client came to the continental United States. After being released from jail, her husband was not allowed to travel because his green card had been taken away. The client talked with his sister and was told that her husband had been in some kind of fiery accident. He is alive but he is badly deformed.

From the group I studied, Hanna exemplifies having the most aftereffects. In November of 2006 she says that she and her oldest daughter had gone to the mall. Hanna saw a man that looked like her ex-husband and she began running. Scenes of the abuse began flashing in her head. Before I used the word trauma, the Hanna explained her situation as traumatic. She shared so many other experiences which made her interview the longest of the participants.

Just as with the other participants, Hanna's children were affected by the domestic violence. When they left St. Croix and she would invite male friends to her home. The children would ask, "Are you going to beat our mommy?" The last relationship the client was in the man began shouting at her. Hanna's younger chil- dren would intervene by letting both their mother and the friend know that they dis- approved of the shouting. Her oldest son, while in St. Croix showed his displeasure by drawing pictures. The drawing was of a tall man and a little boy standing beside him. The little boy had a knife and was stabbing the man in the leg. His teacher had a social worker go to the home to investigate whether something was happening. Hanna expressed that everything was fine. To this day she regrets having not told the truth. Her older son is now in the penal system and is also an abuser.

Listening to their stories reminded of my own experience as a survivor of domestic violence and abuse. As they began sharing their personal testimonies I wanted to cry. Since they were not crying, I held back the tears. Their courage and willingness to share convinced me that I am on the right track. I was inspired to develop a ministry model designed to empower those who are suffering from the aftereffect of abuse. The next chapter includes the method of how I proceeded to help these women and myself through this special project.

CHAPTER THREE

Methodology

❂

Outline of the Ministry Model

The effect of domestic violence does not end with the termination of the rela- tionship between the abused and the perpetrator. The aftereffects or the trauma of the abuse may be felt many years following the experience. After the abuse has ceased, what are some steps leading toward restoration and healing for women who are survivors of domestic violence? What did not happen in the shelter or protective process which caused the women not to receive what they needed to be restored? Why are the women left with the aftereffects?

The aftereffects of domestic violence can stifle a woman's ability to live holis- tically. Her suffering is not through physical pain but through psychological and emotional pain which have not healed because it is not noticeably visible. This lack of visibility is not always blindness on the part of those who may want to help. For various reasons a survivor may masquerade her suffering.

The importance of this ministry is to create an educational model that can be used to help transform and empower survivors who are experiencing the afteref- fects. It is also necessary for the survivors to connect with those who have had similar experiences. "Recovery can take place only within the context of relation- ships; it cannot occur in isolations."[9] Survivors must rid the fear that what they experienced only happened to them.

This ministry model attempted to create an educational tool that included a plat- form on which survivors of domestic violence, who are experiencing the afteref- fects could share what had happened to them. They were allowed to freely tell their story. This time of sharing afforded them the opportunity to witness that they were not alone in their experience. The study also provided a biblically based curriculum which allowed the clients to see how their lives could be transformed through the word of God. It was hoped that this process would educate the women on how to raise their self-esteem. During this potential process of healing, the women were also to be strengthened so that they could help other women by educating them on how to recover from the aftereffects of domestic violence.

To establish the validity of this ministry project the methodology of data tri- angulation was chosen to document the process. I performed a content analysis through the methods of: 1) Observation; 2) Interview; 3) Focus Group. The research methods that were used to test the treatment hypothesis were conducted using qual- itative research design.

---

[9] Judith Herman, *Trauma and Recovery: The Aftermath of Violence-From Domestic Abuse to Political Terror* (New York, NY: Basic Books, 1997), 133.

Hypothesis

The hypothesis for this project is that women who are survivors of domestic violence can be empowered to overcome the aftereffects. The problem of this study is to create a biblically based educational tool. This tool will provide a platform to promote growth to help survivors of domestic violence overcome the aftereffects. This restoration process is necessary even though the woman is no longer involved in the intimate relationship.

Several steps must be taken in order for the survivor to be restored and empow- ered to rise up out of the aftereffects. First, the survivor must be able to tell her story so that she can be free from secrets. Domestic violence has long since been held in secrecy by the victim, the perpetrator, the church and society.

Secondly, in the restoration process, self-esteem must be built on a strong biblical foundation. Mere generic phrases such as "you are beautiful," or "you are capable," are not enough. Women, who are experiencing aftereffects, are not generic. In the restoration process, the healing requires the survivor to jump from the sidelines and reach deeply within herself to get to the root of the hurt.[10]

Restoration is a continuing process but with time and effective care the survivor can become stronger. Finally, once the survivor is on the road to restoration she should be able to encourage other women to start their journey of healing.

Many programs exist to help the victims of domestic vio- lence escape imme- diate danger. Once the victims are safe and out of that relationship they enter a new status from that of victim to that of survivor. The challenge for the survivor is

---

[10] Jeanne Roberts, *I Cry God! Hope and Healing for Survivors of Childhood Abuse* (Oak Harbor, WA: Xlibris, 2003), 172.

processing what happened to them and why did it happen to them. It then becomes necessary for these and similar questions to be processed and answered with the help of outside intervention. This intervention should be designed to educate and bring about awareness for the need of restoration for the survivor.

Intervention

This ministry project consisted of four sessions. The first session was a personal taped recorded interview with each of the participants conducted by me. There were several objectives for the personal recorded interview. The first objective was to listen to the participant talk about her thoughts, feelings and emotions since her domestic violence experience. The second objective was to provide historical infor- mation about the participant and her abusive experience. The third objective was for me to observe the behavior and responses given. The last objective was to allow me to talk about what I had experienced. It was necessary for them to know that they were talking with someone who understood what they were going through. Most of the participants expressed that they had not extensively talked to anyone about their ordeal.

There were three-two hour structured sessions with the group. I suggest that the program be extended to ten to twelve weeks to adequately attempt to complete the healing process. My time was restricted because of the time restraints of the class. The objectives for the group sessions were as follows:

- To allow the client to freely tell her story
- To let the client know that she is not alone in her experience
- To restore the client's self-esteem
- To gain strength to help other victims and survivors overcome the aftereffect of domestic violence

Each session had a specific topic of discussion. The segments of the session were based upon the particular subject of the day's session. The session included the varying combination of testimonials, scripture reading, and three study ques- tions for discussion, role play, videos, tape recordings, articles, CDs litanies, silent reflection, closing prayer and evaluation. The first session's testimonial period focused on the personal interviews. The testimonials for sessions two and three were a reflection of the previous session.

The purposes of the testimonials were to allow the women to share and to listen to each others. Specific scriptures were chosen to establish a biblical foundation so that the women could see that God, through the Word of God, was aware of their situation and that God provides healing. Audio/visual aids were used to increase awareness and to incite discussion. These aids included CD player, cassette tape recorder and DVD player. The curriculum for the sessions was placed in a pocket folder that included the session agenda, articles, reference materials, litany, note paper, an evaluation form to be filled after each meeting and an exit questionnaire. The participants also received a pen, a pencil, and a Bible. Folders were given back to me after each session for review.

The evaluation form was to be filled at the end of each session. The participants were to reflect upon the previous session and be prepared to share at the next session. The final and third session was designed so that the participants would have ample time to share in their group experience.

Closing Thoughts

During the course of this project, confirmation came to me that the ministry needs to be implemented in our communities. On Sunday, March 4, 2007, I had plans of visiting the various Sunday school classes at the church where I served as pastor. My plans were interrupted when a member of the church brought in a young lady into my office. Sheena (not her real name) was crying and thankful that the doors were open. She had just been attacked by her best friend who lived across the street from the church. Sheena said that Brent (not his real name) was following her and that she was terrified that he was going to do her harm.

While in the office, I shared part of my story and assured her that she was safe. I put some men of the church on alert because there had just been a recent incident of a domestic violence dispute that led to a shooting in a Detroit church. I then encouraged Sheena to call the police but her reply was that she did not want to bring shame to her family. She was encouraged to stay for the worship service and during the service she had a traumatized stare in eyes. After the service I took her to her aunt's home. The incident left a haunting feeling in my soul. I thought that I would never see Sheena again but she came to the church the following Tuesday to thank me. Sheena's story made for good conversation during the group sessions. It allowed them to express their feeling about hearing of women who are still involved in abusive relationships.

The final session was rewarding to me and the clients. After the session the par- ticipants in attendance began sharing some closing thoughts about what they had experienced from their weeks together. Amanda said, "I know that this is the last session but this is the last time that I will have to deal with my domestic violence experience." She expressed this because she had been in many abusive relation- ships which began with her uncle attacking her at seven years old. She said that she realizes that she does not have to settle for anybody. She feels that it is important for a woman to get to know herself before getting involved in another relationship. Having a relationship with Jesus Christ has now become a priority with her. She also expressed appreciation for the scriptures that were given during the sessions.

Another revelation Amanda had is that one cannot pick someone up and get them out of a domestic violence situation. I agreed with her that the one being abused has to get tired of the situation. The client asked the question, "How does a person beat another human being like that?" I explained to her that the perpetrator has his target. It is unfortunate that the target is some one who is close to him. The perpetrator does not beat his boss nor abuse his neighbor yet he hurts the one who loves him. It was resolved that the perpetrator must be held accountable for his actions.

As the conversation continued I recited the old adage, "If you do the crime; you must do the time" which is an appropriate action for the perpetrator. For Christians, forgiveness must be granted to those who ask for forgiveness if they repent. Forgiveness is more than just a bandage on a deep wound. There must be some thought given to forgiveness for the perpetrator and the one who has been abused. All of the participants said that they have forgiven their perpetrator. I do not doubt that but after learning more and more about forgiveness I wonder was it given too soon.

Also in that final conversation the participants expressed appreciation for being able to give voice to their experience. They agreed with me that one can not get through the trauma of domestic violence by themselves. Pamela stated that she knew of two prostitutes on the streets of River Rouge who were being abused by their pimp and their solicitors. She said that if this ministry existed, those prosti- tutes could have somewhere to go so that they can talk about what they are going through. Pamela's enthusiasm was so strong that I thought that she was going to leave the session to go get the prostitutes. That was definitely one of the emotions that I was hoping to invoke throughout the implementation of the ministry project. The idea of the project was for women who were once bound by the chains of domestic violence to be set free. In their freedom they would in turn reach back to help another sister to arise and walk.

CHAPTER FOUR

THEORETICAL FOUNDATION

Domestic violence is one of the most dehumanizing acts committed by one person against another. It is a global phenomenon found in many cultures and religions. Great strides are being taken to address the issue of domestic violence. However, too few theologians have addressed the paralyzing aftereffects domestic violence can have upon its victims and survivors. The reason this statement is made is because domestic violence and abuse knows no race, gender, color nor creed. It is not partial to any particular socio-economic background although there has been research to argue differently. The following theological foundation includes many thoughts that encompass the various aspects of domestic violence.

Theological Foundation

What Others Have to Say

Violence against Women and Children, edited by Carol J. Adams and Marie M. Fortune is a theological resource book. Carol J. Adams, a feminist theologian wrote an essay on the writing of Catharine MacKinnon. MacKinnon is also a femi- nist theologian who has been criticized for her writings on sexual victimization. Adams entitled her essay, "MacKinnon's Theory of Sex Inequality." On the sub- ject of "Women's Words about Sexual Victimization Become Oral Pornography", Adams says that, "The woman who speaks about sexual harassment is experienced as part of a pornographic narrative.[11] The thought behind this is that when a woman speaks about her experience it becomes a sexual act.

Mackinnon gives an example of this theology by what happened during the Clarence Thomas hearings. "The more silent he is, the more powerful and credible. But the moment she opens her mouth, her credibility founders. Senators said they were offended by her; President Bush said he felt unclean. The dirt and uncleanli- ness stuck to her. When she spoke truth to power, she was treated like a pig in a parlor. He said these things but she was blamed."[12]

Many victims of domestic violence do not report their experiences. Perhaps the thought of disbelief and discrediting keeps a victim from voicing her pain. One of the purposes of this ministry is to create a platform or give the space where survi- vors of domestic violence can give voice to their experience.

Joanne Carlson Brown and Rebecca Parker in their essay, "For God So Loved the World?" argue that women have been acculturated to accept abuse. They stand on the premise that women have come to believe that they are to suffer because Christianity has as it basis, suffering.[13] I believe that survivors of domestic violence who are suffering from the after-

---

[11] Carol J. Adams and Marie M. Fortune, Violence against Women and Children: A Christian Theological Sourcebook (New Your: Continuum Publishing Company, 1995), 19.

[12] Ibid.

[13] Ibid., 56.

effects of their experience are not suffering for the cause of Jesus Christ. They are suffering because they have been violated at the hands of someone who has committed a crime. My theology is based on the love of a compassionate God who sent God's Son to suffer so that others can be liberated to enjoy the abundant life for which he came.

It is not God's will for people to suffer. Yet, God is with humankind when suf- fering takes place. Victims of domestic violence suffer as they go through the expe- rience. Survivors of domestic violence suffer the aftereffects even when the outside wounds have healed; they suffer on the inside.

An explanation of this internal suffering from the deep wound of domestic vio- lence and other abuse can be found in Dr. Andrew Sung Park's book entitled, From Hurt to Healing: A theology of the Wounded. He contends that the Christian the- ology of sin and repentance is of no comfort to the one who is suffering from abuse. Park says that there is a Korean word that can adequately describe the pain of this deep wound; that word is *han*. "Han is the rupture of the soul caused by abuse, exploitation, injustice, and violence. When the soul is hurt so much, it bursts sym- bolically; it aches. When the aching soul is wounded again by external violence, the victim suffers yet a deeper ache. The wound produced by such repeated abuse and injustice is han in the depths of the soul."[14]

Dr. Park goes on to describe han as an emotional heart attack; it is a fusion of being exposed, depressed, and anger that is brewed on the inside of an individual. "The powerful receive respect, protection, and appreciation, whereas the victim is further violated and denigrated. Once his or her boundary of protection is broken, it is hard for the victim

---

[14] Andrew Sung Park, From Hurt to Healing: A Theology of the Wounded (Nashville, TN: Abingdon Press, 2004), 11-12.

to restore that boundary again.[15] It is my contention that the boundary may be restored through ministry. This may be achieved through the sharing of the survivors' stories with one another. Once they begin giving voice to what happened to then, healing may begin. It is possible for them to realize that they are not alone in their suffering.

The question may be asked, why is there suffering, especially for those who fall prey to the hands of an abuser? Dr. Marie M. Fortune wrote an article entitled, "The Transformation of Suffering: A Biblical Theological Perspective." She says that, "God allows such sinfulness because God has given persons free will and does not intervene when they choose to engage in unrighteous, unjust acts. Other people suffer from the consequences of these acts."[16]

Dr. Fortune places suffering in two categories; voluntary suffering and involun-tary suffering. Voluntary suffering involves making a painful decision that a person makes to accomplish a greater good. An example of voluntary suffering is like that of the civil rights workers during the 1960's. Even though they were beaten, impris- oned, and some of them were put to death, they knew that their suffering was going to bring about liberation for many. Involuntary suffering, on the other hand, is not chosen and does not serve a common good for anyone. Victims and survivors of domestic violence suffer involuntarily. Many of those who suffer ask the question, WHY?[17]

The one who inflicts involuntary suffering upon another must be held accountable for their actions. Not only are they to be held accountable but Jesus says, "And if the same person sins against you seven times a day, and turns back

---

[15] Ibid., 12.

[16] Adams, Violence against Women and Children, 85.

[17] Ibid., 88.

to you seven times and says, 'I repent,' you must forgive."[18] When a survivor of domestic vio- lence goes through the healing process, she must deal with the issue of forgiveness. "Father, forgive them; for they do not know what they are doing"[19] has been the familiar and commonly used theological basis for the survivor toward the perpe- trator. Dr. Nancy Nason-Clark says, "Yet forgiveness does not erase the pain of the past, nor does it deny its implications. Rather when forgiveness is placed within a broader context of the journey from victim to survivor, it is achieved when the pain of the past no longer controls the future and the victim is no longer entrapped in a complicated web of anger and despair."[20]

Saying, "I'm sorry" or "please, forgive me" has been the patch that has been placed on the deep wound of abuse far too long. Many victims of domestic violence have accepted these words only to be abused again and again. Dr. Marie Fortune warns against the temptation to move to quickly towards forgiveness. When this happens grace becomes cheap. She says that there has to be repentance and accountability on behalf of the perpetrators. The perpetrators have to acknowledge their sin against themselves, the ones they hurt, and the community.

Dr. Fortune had the opportunity of interviewing 25 incest offenders during treat- ment. "They said, 'Tell the clergy for us that they should not forgive us so quickly.' Each of them upon arrest had gone to their minister and had been prayed over, "for- given," and sent home. Each of them said it was the worst thing that could have been done for them. That cheap grace had allowed them to continue to deny responsi-

---

[18] Luke 17:4 New Revised Standard Version (NRSV)

[19] Luke 23:34

[20] Nancy Nason-Clark, "When Terror Strikes at Home: The Interface Between Religion and Domestic Violence," *Journal Scientific Study of Religion* 43, no. 3 (Summer 2004): 304.

bility for their abuse of others. It in no way facilitated their repentance or their treatment."[21]

I agree with Dr. Fortune that forgiveness is one of the most precious gifts that religious leaders and Christians can give. However it should not be "timetabled by someone other than the victim and should never be regarded as a guarantee for safety or protection."[22] A victim or survivor of domestic violence should not be forced into immediately accepting words of forgiveness from their abuser.

When an individual ask for forgiveness, repentance needs to have taken place in their heart. "Repentance means changing one's behavior. This is the concrete expression of contrition. If anyone wants to repent of his or her sin he or she must turn back from sin and walk in the right way."[23] True repentance on the part of the abuser comes out of a haunting sense of guilt and shame.

Guilt and shame is not only felt by the perpetrator but the victims and survivors experience this as well. Dr. Park's theology suggests that there is a distinct difference between guilt and shame, yet they overlap. He says, "In general, shame emerges when one is helplessly wronged or hurt by others. Guilt arises when one commits sin or does not do right. The victims of guilt (the offenders) are primarily haunted by an uneasy conscience; the victims of shame (the offended) largely suffer from embar- rassment because they could not defend their own territory."[24] I agree with Dr. Park on the issues of guilt and shame; however I also feel that the offended experiences some feeling of guilt. Survivors of domestic violence who have children may experi- ence

---

[21] Adams, *Violence against Women and Children*, 453.

[22] Nason-Clark, "When Terror Strikes at Home: The Interface Between Religion and Domestic Violence," 305.

[23] Park, *From Hurt to Healing: A Theology of the Wounded*, 77.

[24] Ibid., 35.

guilty feelings if she thinks that she stayed in the relationship too long. Many children have been affected by abuse in their homes; therefore some mothers take the blame and feel that they should have gotten out of the relationship much sooner. The Theological Foundation for this ministry model has been layered with issues such as sexual victimization, the acculturation of the acceptance of abuse, suffering, forgiveness, guilt and shame. In terms of domestic violence, all of these issues can be viewed through a biblical lens.

Biblical Foundation

Abusive behavior is not a new phenomenon; it merely reflects the violent nature of humankind. It affects not only the victim, but the family and society as a whole. There are scriptural references to domestic violence in the Old Testament and refer- ences to healing in the New Testament.

Second Samuel 13 begins with a pending incestuous relationship between Amnon and his beautiful sister Tamar. Tamar and Absalom were David's children by his wife, Maacah. Amnon was David's son by Ahinoam, a Jezreelitess.[25] Amnon is passionately in love with Tamar. Incestuous relationships were forbidden by Levitical law. "Do not have sexual relations with your sister, either your father's daughter or your mother's daughter, whether she is born in the same home or elsewhere."[26]

In the 6-11 verses, Amnon uses deceit in having Tamar summoned by her father David. She has no reason to suspect anything of her brother.[27] Many testimonials have been given by survivors of domestic violence, including myself, as to how the abuser expresses love at the beginning of the

---

[25] 2 Sam. 3:2-3
[26] Lev. 18:19
[27] 2 Sam. 13:8-10

relationship. Not only does the abuser shows love toward the victim but displays it to her family. Once Amnon gets Tamar alone, in verses 12-14, he overpowers her. She pleads with him not to do such a thing because it is socially unacceptable in Israel. Tamar now thinks of herself and tries to reason with him by asking, "What about me? Where can I get rid of my disgrace?" The one being abused often pleads with the abuser. There are times when the victim tries to psychologically persuade the abuser not to do them harm. There are disenchanting thoughts in the minds of vic- tims that they will somehow awaken a bit of conscience in their abuser.[28]

After the rape, in verses 15-19, it states that Amnon's hatred for Tamar is stronger than the love. Despite her urgent pleas, Amnon orders Tamar to be put outside. She does not get to leave in private humiliation but he has her thrown out in disgrace by a servant. Victims of domestic violence suffer from humiliating shame. "Humiliating shame arises as the keenly painful consciousness of something dis- honorable, inappropriate, and outrageously done to a person by another. A victim suffers from the shame of humiliation. The primary causes of this type of shame are transgression and crime."[29]

Verse 20 asserts that Tamar became a desolate woman. Her well-being was not an issue. Her brother Absalom questioned her as to what Amnon had done. But Absalom went on to tell Tamar to be quiet because after all he is her brother. He continued by telling her not to take what happened to her to heart. She becomes empty, alone and grim without anyone recognizing her depression.

The shame she felt as a result of this rape and incest was too great to suppress. Her loud cry, imposition of ashes,

---

[28] Hans W. Hertzberg, I and II Samuel: A Commentary (London: SCM Press LTD, 11964), 324,

[29] Park, From *Hurt to Healing: A Theology of the Wounded*, 38.

and the torn long robe symbolize the double shame of her helplessness and degradation. Her father, knowing what had hap- pened, nonetheless kept silent out of his need to protect his son and successor, Amnon. David's own sense of his self-interest trumped his sense of justice for Tamar, leading his daughter to suffer the triple shame of humiliation: rape, incest and her father's knowing silence.[30]

Tamar's soiled reputation and state of mind affected more than just her. These verses indicate a violation of the family and social structures of Israel. Because of the sacrilege nature of rape, the act itself poses a serious threat to the society. With this happening within the royal family the whole society is affected.

Absalom hated his brother and did not talk with him for two years. He sought revenge as to how to repay him for disgracing their sister. This hatred resulted in Amnon being killed by his brother. Long after the abuse had ceased, the painful affects of domestic violence can be felt by those associated with both the victim and the abuser.

Some survivors of domestic violence suffer from unhealthy feelings, thoughts and emotions brought on as a result of their painful experiences. They fail to fulfill God's will and purpose for their lives because they have been traumatized. I believe that freedom and empowerment can be found in the Word of God.

In Genesis 1:26, God said, "Let us make man in our image, after our likeness."[31] The word man, in Hebrew is '*adam*.'[32] The meaning represents a human being (an individual or the species, mankind). Women are included!

---

[30] Kyle McCarter, Jr., *Anchor Bible: A New Translation wit Introduction, Notes and Commentary of Second Samuel* (New York: Doubleday, 1984).

[31] Gen. 1:26, King James Version (KJV).

[32] *The New Strong Complete Dictionary of Bible Words* (1996), s.v. "Adam."

From a social justice per- spective, every person is fearfully and wonderfully made in the image and likeness of God. Therefore, every individual is precious in God's sight.

The New Testament is layered with many incidents of exploitation, discrimina- tion and sexual victimization of women. The woman taken in adultery in chapter 8 of John was used by the Pharisees to trap Jesus.[33] Passages such as 1 Corinthians 14:33b-36 and 1Timothy 2:11-15 have been used to discriminate against women in leadership in the church.

In chapter 16 of Acts, the girl with the spirit of divina- tion was exploited by the men who used her for their finan- cial gain. Paul and Silas met this young slave girl in Philippi who "had a spirit by which she predicted the future."[34] The Anchor Bible says that this girl had a gift of prophecy.

Domestic violence has no boundaries when it comes to the women it affects. The slave girl represents all women for she was not given a name. The one thing she had been given was a gift from God that had been abused by greedy men who profited from her. Philippi was a trade center which may explain the presence of Lydia and the dying and selling of purple. The city was therefore visited by many of whom the men sought ways in which to make money. "During their time with Lydia, Paul and his companions encountered a slave girl with a *spirit of divination* whose fortune-telling was very lucrative for her owners. She rightly identified the missionaries as *slaves of the Most High God, who pro- claim to you a way of salva- tion.* After many days of this, Paul commanded the spirit to leave the girl, reminis- cent of Jesus' exorcisms."[35]

---

[33] John 8:3-11.

[34] Act 16:16-19

[35] Watson Mills and Richard F. Wilson, *Mercer Commentary on the Bible* (Macon, GA: Mercer University Press, 1995), 1107.

Domestic violence and abuse is an evil which needs to be exorcised from society. Just like the slave girl many women in abusive relationships are bound to a situation in which they can not see their way out. For various reasons such as fear, shame, hopelessness, insecurity, and low self esteem victims feel trapped in a situation of which there seems to be no escape. The girl with the spirit of divination probably experienced what Nancy Nason-Clark and Catherine Clark Koeger calls and unhealthy relationship.

- You are belittled, and your value and your accomplishments are not recog- nized.
- You are threatened.
- You are slapped, pushed, kicked or hurt.
- You are kept away from your family and friends.
- There is extreme possessiveness or jealousy.
- Your partner insists on being together all the time, or on monitoring what you do when you are alone.
- You, your family, your work, your church and your friends are disrespected.
- You are ignored when you give an opinion, your likes and dislikes count for nothing.
- You are called names that are embarrassing and hurtful.
- You are blamed for all the problems.[36]

The slave girl could not set herself free without the intervention of Paul and Silas who did not turn away from her but relieved her. It is through the interven- tion of others that victims of domestic violence can be set free. This intervention includes programs, ministries, and legislation on the part of

---

[36] Nancy Nason-Clark and Catherine Clark Kroeger, *Refuge from Abuse: Healing and Hope for Abused Christian Women* (Downers Grove, IL: Inter Varsity Press, 2004), 8.

political activist who will not turn their heads away from the reality of the atrocity of domestic violence.

The men in Philippi made a profit off of the slave girl. Once she was set free they blamed Paul and Silas for bringing about strange customs that disturbed the city. Who stands to profit from domestic violence and abuse? If it can be called a profit it would be the perpetrators. Their need to exert power and control over their victims is a gain in their eyes. When they are exposed they place the blame every- where else except upon themselves. Most abusers blame the victims for having to be treated in such a manner.

After the exorcism Paul and Silas are dragged into the forum before the mag- istrates, stripped, beaten with rods and placed into the dungeon of the prison over night. These were the consequences of setting the slave girl free. What a price they paid for a stranger. Just as Paul and Silas suffered consequences for helping this young girl, there is also a cost in helping victims of domestic violence.

Paul and Silas represent the church and others who speak out against domestic violence and abuse. It is difficult to oppose institutions and cultures that have been accepting of this behavior. Domestic violence has been around for centuries; this will be discussed in more detail in the Historical Foundation.

The church is the one institution that a victim of domestic violence can seek refuge. I believe that this is still true. Unfortunately there have been individuals who have taken the word of God and misconstrued it to support their desire to continue permitting domestic violence and abuse. A good example is taking those scriptures that pertain to slavery and submission and using them to subvert the minds of helpless victims. Those who speak out against the misuse of scripture are said to be womanist, feminist and liberators who come with a strange doctrine.

Another cost for advocates is their time and persistence for the cause. Helping victims, survivors and all who are associated with them is an ongoing process. Individuals and organizations must be committed to the cause of liberation. The sacrifice of time and resources are necessary for helping victims. If Paul and Silas had not done what they did for the slave girl there is no telling as to her fate.

There is even a greater cost if something is not done about domestic violence and abuse. Too many victims do not live to become survivors. The children who are involved are often abused by the perpetrator. Not on that, but children are affected in so many other ways. If they do not grow up to become the abused they some- times become the abuser.

The consequences that Paul and Silas suffered were short lived. Their stay in prison was overnight. It must be remembered than an entire household was saved because of the price that Paul and Silas paid. This is encouraging to those who are involved in the liberation of individuals who are suffering from domestic vio- lence and abuse. All who are involved in these types of situations can benefit. This includes the perpetrator.

From the Old to the New Testaments, the Bible teaches that an individual should love their neighbor as they love themselves. Survivors of domestic violence may have a hard time loving themselves or have a low opinion of themselves because of the ridiculing and criticizing that they heard from their abuser. Self-love is therefore important for the sur- vivor to learn. Recognizing the unconditional love that God showed Humankind by sending God's son is a major move toward self-love.

In chapter 5 of the Book of Mark, Jesus is summoned by the father of a young girl who is very ill. As He was going to see about the girl, he was interrupted. In the crowd was a woman who had been bleeding for twelve years. She spent all of her money going from doctor to doctor only to get worse. She determined in her mind that if she could just touch Jesus' cloak she would be healed. Immediately, her bleeding stopped and she knew that she had been healed.

Jesus realized that some power had left and wanted to know who touched him. His disciples could not believe that he would be asking such a question in a pressing crowd. When the woman recognized what had happened to her she came trembling and knelt at Jesus' feet. She then told him her story. Jesus told her that her faith had healed her and to go in peace.

A woman suffering from a bleeding disorder was considered ceremonially unclean. She was not allowed in public. In the case of the woman in the text, twelve years was a long time to be isolated from family and the community.

Women who are victims of domestic violence experience times of isolation. The abuser often tries to keep the one he is abusing close by. The focus of this ministry however, is on the effects of domestic violence even when the abuser is out of the picture. Some women go through periods of isolation which is a sign of depression and other emotional disorders.

Returning to the text in Mark 5, the girl died. Death is not a challenge for the power of God. When Jesus arrived at the home, he put all of the mourners out. He took her by the hand and said, *"Talitha cumi*; which is, being interpreted, Damsel, I say unto thee, arise."[37]

The subtitle of this book is Empowering Women to Rise Up: A Ministry for the Aftereffects of Domestic Violence and Abuse. The girl in the Mark 5 passage was not a victim of domestic violence. However, she was in an immobilized state. Upon her awakening, Jesus requests that she be given something to eat. Domestic violence places a woman in a lying down state of mind and spirit. It is our Lord's desire for women of abuse to get up and return to life. It is through the

---

[37] Mark 5:41 (KJV)

church and other entities that victims of domestic violence are to be nourished and restored.

The August 2007 Intensive of United Theological Seminary of Trotwood, OH was entitled, "Women in Ministry: Reconcilers, Reformers and Revolutionaries." One of the speakers for the week was Bishop Charlene Payne Kammerer of the United Methodist Church. Bishop Kammerer chose for her text Matthew 15:22-28, the story of the Canaanite woman who sought healing from Jesus for her demon possessed daughter. Jesus had no response for the woman who was being urged away by the disciples. Jesus then explained to her that he was sent for the lost sheep of Israel. In spite of being referred to as a dog, the woman was persistent in her plea. Because of her faith, Jesus answered her request.

As Bishop Kammerer expounded upon the text, I began seeing it through the lens of domestic violence. She said that Jesus was struggling as to what to do in his ministry.[38]

Jesus can be seen in the first part of the story as the attitude of the church. The church tends to want to take care of its own. It has the propensity to not want to go beyond the walls to help others. From time to time, the church as been inclined to turn its face away from the reality of social ills and not get involved in social justice and political activism.

The church struggles as to what to do about the issue of domestic violence for various reasons:

1. Domestic violence is happening in the church. Abusers and the abused are in the church and the crime is sometimes committed by church leaders.
2. There is confusion in the interpretation of scripture. Scriptures on submis- sion such as, "Wives, submit

---

[38] Charlene Kammerer, "Wednesday Worship Service-D.Min. Intensive" (Lecture, United Theological Seminary, Trotwood, OH, 15 August 2007).

yourselves unto your own husband" has been used to validate abuse.[39]

Bishop Kammerer said that the woman changed Jesus' understanding of his mis- sion and ministry by God.[40] The church needs to rethink its mission and ministries to help those who are victims and survivors of domestic violence. The Canaanite woman can be seen as those who want to help victims and survivors of abuse. Those who want to help are sometimes rejected by the church because of the his- tory of the acceptance of domestic violence within the church.

Survivors and victims are unlikely to speak up for themselves. They need someone who will go before God and the powers that be, on their behalf. They too are invited to the table of the Lord where they have a voice.

The Canaanite woman was persistent in her request for healing for her daughter. Advocates for domestic violence have to be persistent in seeking social justice and political action on behalf of victims and survivors. The church along with advo- cates for justice should kneel before God to ask for a blessing for someone else. Unlike David who ignored his daughter Tamar, this Canaanite woman sought help for her daughter.

Once the process of restoration and healing begins the victim becomes a sur- vivor. It is God's plan for the survivor to be strengthened during the process of healing. It was most unfortunate and cruel for Tamar to be left desolate. Her story went on without her being present and without her receiving the inheritance that God has for God's children. Tamar never knew about Jesus. He is the advantage that survivors of domestic violence have today.

---

[39] Eph. 5:22; Col. 3:18
[40] Charlene Kammerer, "Wednesday Worship Service-D.Min. Intensive."

In chapter 1 of Colossians, Paul refers to the entitlement of the inheritance for the saints of the kingdom of light. "Having a portion in the inheritance of the saints means being transposed into the kingdom (basileia) of the beloved who is placed in opposition to the realm of darkness."[41] For Christians, darkness represents the kingdom that is ruled by Satan. Domestic violence is part of that kingdom but the survivor has been rescued. Paul told the Colossians, "For he has rescued us from the dominion of darkness and brought us into the kingdom of the Son he loves, in whom we have redemption, the forgiveness of sins."[42] This rescue is not something that has to take place in the future; it has already taken place because God has already delivered. This deliverance is from all kinds of circumstances such as per- secution, death, and even abuse.

A survivor of domestic violence has been set free from their abuser's physical assaults. However, the emotional pain will continue if the survivor is not told and shown the love and redemption of God. She has to accept and receive the redemp- tive work that God has done on her behalf through grace.

Historical Foundation

The focus of this ministry is to empower women by educating them, using scripture to help them rise up out of the aftereffects of domestic violence and abuse. Members of the congregations who will be involved in the ministry of empowering women need to be informed of the gravity and history of domestic violence in society.

---

[41] Markus Barth and Helmut Blanke, *The Anchor Bible: A New Translation with Introduction and Commentary: Colossians* (New York: Doubleday, 1994), 187.

[42] Col. 1:13-14

Wife beating has been around for many centuries. The image of the cave man dragging his woman with one hand and holding a club in the other indicates soci- ety's thoughts as to how long this behavior has existed. Male violence toward women and children existed in ancient Rome and Greece. The order of priority for a man was father, cattle, mother and then children. With this hierarchy, it is understandable as to why a man would consider his family as his property.[43]

Jesus Christ taught total equality in spite of the Jewish tradition of female sub- jection. A line in a prayer spoken by a Jewish man daily is: "I thank God that He did not make me a Gentile, a slave, or a woman."[44] With such a prayer, one could understand Paul's statement in Galatians 3:38 that, "There is neither Jew nor Greek, slave nor free, male nor female, for you are all one in Christ Jesus." This indicates that a woman was a person and not just a piece of property.

The controlling attitude filtered into the European society. Women were viewed as needing strict control. During the medieval period, the church had clergy who taught that husbands had a right and an obligation to beat their wives. "Rules of Marriage," written by Friar Cherubino is a good example of the teaching of the times. He stated that if a husband's verbal correction of his wife was not effective, then he was to "...take up a stick and beat her, not in rage, but out of charity and concern for her soul, so that the beating will rebound to your merit and her good."[45]

The Renaissance and Reformation periods brought about social, political and religious changes. However by the sixteenth century there was little change toward the treatment of

---

[43] Grant L. Martin, *Counseling for Family Violence and Abuse* (Waco, TX,: Word Books, 1987), 22.

[44] Ibid.

[45] Ibid., 23.

women. Martin Luther is said to have made a statement while boasting about his successful marriage that when his wife became 'saucy' all she received was a 'box on the ear.'"[46] The attitude of permitting a man to strike his wife is an unfortunate American tradition. It was accepted as a man's right to beat a woman. Even with the accep- tance, there were those political activist who fought to break the tradition of domestic violence.

The Massachusetts Bay Colony established a rule in 1655, that if a man beat his wife, he was fined a maximum of ten pounds and/or given corporal punishment. By 1870, the same year that the Christian Methodist Episcopal Church was founded, Massachusetts and Alabama began to reject the legal justification of wife beating.[47]

Many states began granting one spouse permission to divorce another based upon abuse. However by 1910, there were still eleven states that would not grant a divorce based upon domestic violence.

It cannot be discounted that African men and women endured horrible condi- tions during the years of the slave trade. Molefi Asante writes, quoting Hoschshild, "What happens to all of the women who are taken prisoners? Some are set free when their husbands have done all they can to regain the one who is dearest to them. Others are forced to work in the fields and also to work as prostitutes. Our most respected men here have told us with tears in their eyes and much vexation in their hearts that they had recently seen a group of seven hundred women chained together and transported to the coast on steamboats…So can anyone feel truly surprised that the discontent has finally come to the surface?[48]

---

[46] Ibid., 24.
[47] Ibid., 26.
[48] Molefi Kete Asante, *The History of Africa: The Quest for Eternal Harmony* (New York: Routledge Taylor & Francis Group, 2007), 228.

Consideration must be given that slavery in America has some bearing on domestic violence in the African American community. According to Edward Wimberly, "Abuse is the attempt to gain a sense of meaning and value at the expense of the growth and well-being of another."[49] Many theories have surfaced as to why African American men respond to being devalued with violence. How African American women respond to being devalued need to be examined. African American men and women have internalized the devaluation of African American women by society as a whole.

It is most unfortunate when the devaluation of an African American woman is exercised by an African American man. This is reflective of what happened during the Anita Hill-Clarence Thomas hearing is October 1991. Rosemary L. Bray writes, "By Sunday evening, Anita Hill's testimony lay buried under an avalanche of insin- uation and innuendo. Before the eyes of the nation a tenured law professor beloved by her students was transformed into an evil, opportunistic harpy; a deeply reli- gious Baptist was turned into a sick and delusional woman possessed by Satan and in need of exorcism, this youngest of thirteen children from a loving family became a frustrated spinster longing for attention of her fast-track superior, bent on exacting a cruel revenge for his rejection."[50]

Domestic violence is a festering crime that thrives off of the power and control of an individual who cannot deal with his or her own inadequacies and insecurities. Several years prior to the Anita Hill-Clarence Thomas hearings activist had been on the march against domestic violence and abuse.

---

[49] Wimberly, *Counseling African and American Families*, 112.

[50] Carol J. Adams and Marie M. Fortune, "Taking Sides against Ourselves," *Violence against Women and Children* (New York: Continuum, 1995), 363.

The same beliefs and cultural norms that promoted the subjugation of women over the years have also promoted advocacy against it. Some of the benchmarks of change occurred during the time that I was living in an abusive relationship. The movement during the 1970's brought about public awareness of domestic violence issues. "In 1974, the first shelter for battered women was established. Opening the shelter led to the establishment of hundreds of shel- ters and domestic violence programs throughout the United States. These programs provide emotional, financial, and vocational assistance to domestic violence survi- vors and their children. Sometimes legal assistance and support is even provided."[51]

It was also during the 1970's that police officers were taught to respond dif- ferently to calls related to domestic violence. Previously they went into a situation only to bring about peace and leave saying, "You all behave yourselves." It was during this same time period that officers responded to reports of Domestic distur- bances differently than other calls. They would get the stories separately of those involved and tried to treat the situation with band-aids. They talked with the parties involved by trying to calm them down so that they would not have to return again. The officers threatened them with arrest if they had to return.

Twenty years later during the 1990's domestic violence was treated as a serious problem. They no longer merely threatened the parties involved but they began arresting. Their responses were not just peacemaking efforts but they were saving live. Some state laws were enacted that held police personally liable if they failed to arrest, and it resulted

---

[51] Peter Moser, *The History of Domestic Violence: Early Days of Domestic Violence, Police Intervention, Court Rulings*, available from http://abuse.suite101.com/article.cfm/the_history_of_domestic_violence. (Accessed 10 October 2007).

in a victim later being killed or injured. Those states fined an officer $1000 who failed to follow the new regulations. Temporary Restraining Orders were issued by the officers if the court was not opened. If an individual vio- lated the restraining order they could be held without bail.

The effect of domestic violence can be felt not only by the victim and the per- petrator but it infiltrates the whole community. This crime continues to be misun- derstood by society as a problem in relationships. Until recently, domestic violence in the home was considered a private affair between the parties involved. Law enforcement did not want to get involved in domestic calls because of the uncer- tainty of the situation.

During the past twenty years, changes have been made by advocates with social justice and political activism. Laws to protect victims along with stiffer penalties and sentences for the perpetrators have also been enacted.

From its beginning in 1870, the Christian Methodist Episcopal Church desired to preach good news, teach divine truth and heal the brokenness of life by the power of God in Jesus Christ. The Social Creed in the Book of Discipline of the Christian Methodist Episcopal Church 2002 states:

> The concern of the Christian Methodist Episcopal Church for the social well-being of humankind springs from the act of God in Jesus Christ as revealed in the Gospel, and from the life and witness of John Wesley and other fathers of Methodism who minis- tered to the physical, intellectual, and social needs of the people to whom they preached the gospel of personal redemption.
>
> The interest activity of the C.M.E. Church in the improvement of human condition parallels the very history of our Church. In the opening edito- rial

of the Gospel Trumpet published in 1897, Bishop Lucius Holsey stated that its purpose would be to "discuss without hesitation, any phase of the civic, social, and those economic and political questions that may affect the well-being of the Church and race." This policy of active participation in the solution of social problems has not been restricted to literary and jour- nalistic endeavor. It can be seen in the individual contribution of some of the leaders of our church during its history – Lucius H. Holsey, Isaac Lane, C.H. Phillips, Randal A. Carter, J.A. Hamlett, J.A. Bray, J.A. Martin, and Channing H. Tobias. It can be seen in those official programs and practices of the local, regional and national levels that were designed to eradicate crime, disease, ignorance, poverty and racial injustice. It has been demon- strated by unknown thousands who are members of the Christian Methodist Episcopal Church as they have resisted oppression and pursued liberty and justice for all humankind.[52]

In the Old Testament of the Bible, Proverbs 21:25 states, "When justice is done, it brings joy to the righteous but terror to evildoers." I found joy almost twenty years ago. At that time I divorced my husband who abused me both physically and emotionally from the time I was married in December 1975.

---

[52] William E. George, *The Book of Discipline of the Christian Methodist Episcopal Church 2006* (Memphis, TN: C.M.E. Publishing House, 2006), 28.

CHAPTER FIVE

STATISTICS OF DOMESTIC VIOLENCE IN THE UNITED STATES

The statistics regarding domestic violence are alarming. In the United States nearly one third of women reported being abused by a husband or boyfriend at some point in their lives. Each year, between one and three million women, are physically, sexually, or mentally abused. Over 1700 women are murdered by their intimate partner. The victim and the perpetrator are not the only ones affected. At least 10 million children are exposed to this behavior in their homes. Approximately 50 percent of men who assault their wives assault their children.[53]

Domestic violence is all-encompassing in Michigan and across the United States. According to the Michigan Resource Center on Domestic and Sexual Violence, nearly 25 percent of surveyed women and 7.6 percent of surveyed

---

[53] Elaine J. Alpert, Al Miles, and Vickii Coffey, Responding to Domestic Violence: An Interfaith Guide to Prevention and Intervention (Chicago, IL: Chicago Metropolitan Battered Women's Network, 2005), 12.

men said that they were raped and/or physically assaulted by a current or former spouse, cohab- iting partner, or date at some time in their lifetime. Women experience higher rates than men of both fatal and non-fatal violence by an intimate partner. Approximately 4.8 million intimate partner rapes and physical assaults are perpetrated against U.S. women annually compared to approximately 2.9 million intimate partner physical assaults against U.S. men annually.[54] Seventy-eight percent of stalking victims are women. Eighty one percent of women who were stalked by a current or former husband or cohabiting partner were also physically assaulted by their partner and 31 percent were also sexually assaulted by the same partner.[55] In 2004, Detroit reported more than 26,000 cases of domestic violence. Every 15 seconds a woman is battered.

The Michigan Domestic Violence Prevention and Treatment Board publish a Domestic Violence Homicide Listing. The information is made up of newspaper stories. It is estimated that more than 100 domestic violence related homicides occur each year in Michigan, yet the list contains information on less than half that number, as newspapers do not cover all domestic violence homicides.

In the city of River Rouge, the city where I resided when I started my project, there are no places of refuge for women who are seeking shelter from a domestic violence relationship. At the time of this writing, there are only two in metro Detroit. There are various women ministries in the area that addressed the issue of domestic violence. However, there are not enough aggressive programs and min- istries designed by the church to help these women to over come the aftereffects.

---

[54] U.S. Department of Justice, *Stalking in America: Findings from the National Violence against Women Survey*, April 1998). Pamphlet.
[55] Ibid.

APPENDICES

Empowering Women to Rise Up: Ministry for the Aftereffects of Domestic Violence and Abuse

Domestic Violence and Abuse Questionnaire

                                  YES NO SOMETIMES

1. Are you still intimately involved with your abuser?

2. How long have you been out of that intimate relationship?

3. Did you grow up in an abusive home?

4. Do you have children with your abuser?

5. Have you been in another intimate relationship with some one other than the abuser?

Domestic Violence and Abuse Questionnaire, *continued*

YES NO SOMETIMES

6. If you answered YES to question 5, are there any similarities between him and your abuser?

7. Are you easily frightened or jumpy?

8. Do you visualize or have unwanted thoughts about your abusive relationship?

9. Do you have dreams or nightmares about your abusive relationship?

10. Does it bother you to watch movies or see re-enactments of domestic violence?

11. When you see your abuser or someone who resembles him, do you get sweaty palms, fast heart rate or nervous?

12. Do you avoid talking about your abu- sive relationship?

13. Even though you may share some of your experiences, is there still some- thing that you cannot or choose not to talk about?

Domestic Violence and Abuse Questionnaire, *continued*

                                                      YES NO SOMETIMES

14. Do you feel shame about what hap- pened to you?

15. Are you angry with yourself and/or others?

16. Do you feel that the abuse was your fault?

17. Have you forgiven your abuser?

18. Do you choose to be alone as oppose to being around others?

19. Have you ever used alcohol or nar- cotics to dull the pain?

20. Did you ever have thoughts of suicide during or since your abuse?

21. Have you ever received counseling for your domestic violence and abuse experience?

Empowering Women to Rise Up: Ministry for the Aftereffects of Domestic Violence and Abuse

Session 1
Responsive Healing Litany

Leader: O LORD, you brought us up from the grave; you spared us from going down into the pit. (Ps. 30:3 NIV)

Response: **God wants to bring us out of the aftereffects of domestic violence into the healing we need. God wants to set us free.**

Leader: You hear, O LORD, the desire of the afflicted; you encourage them, and you listen to their cry. (Ps. 10:17 NIV)

Response: **For there is nothing covered that will not be revealed, nor hidden that will not be known. Therefore whatever you have spoken in the dark will be heard in the light, and what you have spoken in the ear in inner rooms will be proclaimed on the housetops. (Luke 12:2-3 NKJV) God wants to set us free.**

Leader: Is there no balm in Gilead? Is there no physician there? Why then is there no healing for the wound of my people? (Jer. 8:22 NIV)

All: **There is a balm in Gilead. I am healed. I am whole. God has set me free and whom the Son sets free is free indeed.**

Empowering Women to Rise Up: Ministry for the Aftereffects of Domestic Violence and Abuse

Session 1
Overcoming Aftereffects

I. Introduction of the Facilitator and Group Members (15 minutes)
   A. Prayer and Welcome
   B. Purpose of the Group
      1. Distribute folders
      2. Discuss the purpose and contents of the folder
      3. Anonymity
   C. Testimonials (2-3 sentence statements as to why you are here)

II Give the topic of today's session; Overcoming Aftereffects (30 minutes include 10 minute break)
   A. Read Philippians 4:13, Romans 8:15, 2 Timothy 1:7 and John 8:32
   B. 3 study questions pertaining to overcoming after effects
      1. What things have I accomplished since my abuse?
      2. In there any bondage in my life that pertains to or stems from my domestic violence abuse experience?
      3. Am I crying out to God to release me from this bondage?
   C. Silent Reflection
   D. Break

III. Discussion of the 3 questions (1 hour)
   A. Read a portion of the article, "If I Could Close My Eyes"[56]

IV. Closure (15 minutes)
   A. Responsive Healing Litany
   B. Completion of Evaluation Form
   C. Prayer Request
   D. Closing Prayer

---

[56] Esman, Abigail R. "If I Could Close My Eyes, A story of love, pain, hope, and release." *Diane, The Curves Magazine*, Fall 2006, 34.

Empowering Women to Rise Up: Ministry for the Aftereffects of Domestic Violence and Abuse

Session 2
Discovering You by Trusting in God

I. Introduction of the Facilitator and Group Members (15 minutes)
   A. Prayer and Welcome
   B. Purpose of the Group
      1. Distribute folders
      2. Discuss the purpose and contents of the folder
      3. Anonymity
   C. Testimonials (2-3 sentence statements as to why you are here)

II. Give topic of today's session: Discovering You by Trusting in God (30 min- utes include 10 minute break)
   A. Read Matthew 6:25-34, Psalm 55:22-23 and Mark 15:21-28
   B. Watch DVD of screen play[57]
   C. 3 study questions pertaining to discovering you by trusting in God
      1. Do you trust God to handle the aftereffects of your domestic violence and abuse experience?
      2. Have any major changes occurred in your social life since you have been on your own? If so, what are they?
      3. Are you ready to enter into another relationship?
   D. Silent Reflection
   E. Break

---

[57] Ted K. Sims, "Never Say Never," A Musical Gospel Stage Play T & G Productions 2007, DVD.

III. Discussion of the 3 questions and DVD (1 hour)
   A. Listen to a CD by Dianne Reeves, "Testify"[58]

IV. Closure (15 minutes)
   A. Responsive Healing Litany
   B. Completion of Evaluation Form
   C. Prayer Request
   D. Closing prayer

---

[58] Dianne Reeves, "Testify" *In the Moment Live in Concert* [Live], Blue Note Records 2000, compact disc.

Empowering Women to Rise Up: Ministry for the Aftereffects of Domestic Violence and Abuse

Session 2
Responsive Healing Litany

Leader: I will not worry about my life, because God supplies all of my needs.

Response: **My faith in God gives me strength when I need it most. Leader:** My faith makes me strong when I feel weak inside.

Response: **I have the choice t make good decisions for me and my family. My faith in God gives me strength when I need it most.**

Leader: If I delight myself in God, the desires of my heart will be given to me.[59]

Response: **My heart, my mind and my soul belongs to God. My faith in God gives me strength when I need it most.**

All: **I am no longer a victim, I am a survivor. My faith in God gives me strength when I need it most.**

---

[59] Psalm 37:3-6 NIV

Empowering Women to Rise Up: Ministry for the Aftereffects of Domestic Violence and Abuse

Final Session 3
Sharing My Story

I. Introduction of the Facilitator and Group Members (5 minutes)
   A. Prayer and Welcome
      1. Distribute folders
      2. Discuss the contents of the folder
      3. Anonymity

II. Give the topic of today's session: Sharing My Story (1 hour and 30 minutes) A. Listen to Cassette Recording of ABC's Diane Sawyer[60]

III. Closure (25 minutes)
   A. Reaction
      1. Testimonials
      2. Responsive Healing Litany
   B. Completion of Evaluation Forms
   C. Closing Prayer

---

[60] Susan Still, "Domestic Violence Interview," interview by Diane Sawyer, 20/20 Television (October 27, 2006).

Empowering Women to Rise Up: Ministry for the Aftereffects of Domestic Violence and Abuse

Final Session
Sharing My Story

Leader: Faith in God helps to ease the pain that a believer faces.

Response: My faith is strengthened when I hear a sister share her story.

Leader: Sharing the pain and the hope sometimes will lift the burden.[61]

Response: My strength is renewed when I hear a sister share her story.

Leader: Listening to someone else's story may resort your faith in God.

Response: Sharing my story and knowing that I am heard renews my strength day by day.

Leader: When you share your testimony healing can begin.

Response: As I heal, I will be able to share my story so that I can help others.

All: Sharing my story and knowing that I am heard renews my strength day by day. Because I have waited on the Lord, I will soar on wings like eagles. I will run and not grow weary. I will walk and not faint![62]

---

[61] Nancy Nason-Clark and Catherine Clark Kroeger, Refuge from Abuse, Healing and Hope for Abused Christian Women (Inter Varsity Press, 2004). 145.

[62] Isaiah 40:31, NIV

Empowering Women to Rise Up: Ministry for the Aftereffects of Domestic Violence and Abuse

Statement of Anonymity

I _____, do hereby promise that the conver-
  _{Print Your Full Name}
sations we have during these peer sessions will be held in the strictest of confidence. I agree that everything that will be discussed during our peer sessions will remain within the confines of our group sessions. I agree to hold the information provided during the peer sessions in strict confidence.

_____
Print Your Name

_____
Signature

_____
Date

DOMESTIC VIOLENCE AND ABUSE EXIT QUESTIONNAIRE

Project Title: Empowering Women to Rise Up: A Ministry for the Aftereffects of Domestic Violence and Abuse

Researcher: Reverend Janice D. Blackmon
Mentors: Reverend Ivan Douglas Hicks, Ph.D., and Reverend Claude Alexander, D.Min.

This questionnaire will be used to help obtain additional knowledge about your domestic violence and abuse experience after your participation in the project. A response to each question is required as follows: YES, NO, or SOMETIMES. You are asked to provide an explanation for questions 9 and 10. Please circle your responses. If you have any questions about this document please the researcher. When you are finished, please return the questionnaire to the researcher. Your iden- tity will be kept in strict confidence and be protected. You will be assigned a code number which will be placed on this document. The questionnaire will be stored by the researcher.

1. **Would you recommend this ministry to your family and friends?**

    YES   NO   SOMETIMES

2. **Would you participate in a ministry to help victims or survivors of domestic violence and abuse?**

    YES   NO   SOMETIMES

3. Would you be interested in learning how to facilitate this ministry?

        YES   NO   SOMETIMES

4. Are you able to talk with your abuser about the domestic violence?

        YES   NO   SOMETIMES

5. Can you talk with your children about your domestic violence experience?

        YES   NO   SOMETIMES

6. Do you feel that you are ready for another relationship?

        YES   NO   SOMETIMES

7. Are you currently in a relationship?

        YES   NO   SOMETIMES

8. If you are in a relationship, do you make decisions concerning the relationship?

        YES   NO   SOMETIMES

9. Are you happy with you? Explain.

        YES   NO   SOMETIMES

10. Are you more aware of your feelings when involved with decision making with your children and others? Explain.

        YES   NO   SOMETIMES

Session Format

The general format of the sessions was as follows:

I. Introduction of the Facilitator and Group Members (15 minutes).
   A. Prayer and Welcome.
   B. Purpose of the Group.
      1. Distribute folders.
      2. Discuss the purpose and contents of the folder.
      3. Anonymity.
   C. Testimonials (two-three sentence statements as to why you are here).

II. Give the topic of today's session (30 minutes include 10 minute break).
   A. Read Scriptures.
   B. Three Study questions that pertain to the topic.
      1.
      2.
      3.
   C. Silent Reflection
   D. Break.

III. Discussion of the three questions. (1 hour).
   A. Read an article, view video, listened to a CD or tape recording.

IV. Closure (15 minutes).
   A. Responsive Healing Litany.
   B. Completion of Evaluation Forms. C. Prayer Request.
   D. Closing Prayer.

Empowering Women to Rise Up: Ministry for the Aftereffects of Domestic Violence and Abuse

Domestic Violence and Abuse Questionnaire

YES NO SOMETIMES

1. Are you still intimately involved with your abuser?

2. How long have you been out of that intimate relationship?

3. Did you grow up in an abusive home?

4. Do you have children with your abuser?

5. Have you been in another intimate relationship with some one other than the abuser?

6. If you answered YES to question 5, are there any similarities between him and your abuser?

7. Are you easily frightened or jump?

8. Do you visualize or have unwanted thoughts about your abusive relationship?

Domestic Violence and Abuse Questionnaire, *continued*

                                                                   YES NO SOMETIMES

9. Do you have dreams or nightmares about your abusive relationship?

10. Does it bother you to watch movies or see re-enactments of domestic violence?

11. When you see your abuser or someone who resembles him, do you get sweaty palms, fast heart rate or nervous?

12. Do you avoid talking about your abusive relationship?

13. Even though you may share some of your experiences, is there still something that you cannot or choose not to talk about?

14. Do you feel shame about what happened to you?

15. Are you angry with yourself and/or others?

16. Do you feel that the abuse was your fault?

Domestic Violence and Abuse Questionnaire, *continued*

                                                          YES NO SOMETIMES

17. Have you forgiven your abuser?

18. Do you choose to be alone as oppose to being around others?

19. Have you ever used alcohol or nar- cotics to dull the pain?

20. Did you ever have thoughts of suicide during or since your abuse?

21. Have you ever received counseling for your domestic violence and abuse experience?

Empowering Women to Rise Up: Ministry for the Aftereffects of Domestic Violence and Abuse

Session Evaluation Form

	Strongly Disagree				Strongly Agree	Comments
	1	2	3	4	5	

1. Scriptures were relevant to my situation.

2. Facilitator allowed me to ask questions.

3. Sharing my experience made me feel comfortable.

4. Facilitator involved participant.

5. Facilitator demonstrated knowledge of the subject.

6. Session materials were helpful.

BIBLIOGRAPHY

Adams, Carol J. and Marie M. Fortune. *Violence Against Women and Children: A Christian Theological Sourcebook.* New York: Continuum, 1995.

_____. "When the Abuser is Among Us: One Church's Response to a Perpetrator." *Working Together Newsletter.* (Winter 1993/Spring 1994): 1-4. Available from: http://www.faithtrustinstitute.org.

Albright, William F. and C.S. Mann. *The Anchor Bible: Volume 31.* Garden City, NY: Doubleday and Company, Inc. 1981.

Alpert, Al Miles and Vickii Coffey. *Responding to Domestic Violence: An Interfaith Guide to Prevention and Intervention.* Chicago: The Chicago Metropolitan Battered Women's Network, 2005.

Asante Molefi Kete. *The History of Africa: The Quest for Eternal Harmony.* New York: Routledge Taylor and Francis Group, 2007.

Baker, Linda. Wayne County Family Violence Handbook (Detroit, Michigan: Wayne County Department of Children and Family Services, 2005).

Bancroft, Lundy. *Why Does He Do That?* New York: G.P. Putnam's Sons Publishers, 2002.

Blackmon, Janice D. He *Just Might Be Your Angel* (Birmingham, AL: Professionals for Christ Ministries & Publication, 1994).

_____. *The Visitor*, Birmingham, AL: Professionals for Christ Ministries & Publication, 1995.

_____. "Christian Missionaries Helping Victims of Domestic Violence." *The Christian Index*, no. 139 (November 2006): 20.

Brewster Susan. *To Be an Anchor in the Storm: A Guide for Families and Friends of Abused Women*. New York: Ballantine Books, 1997.

Brown, Lou, Francois Dubau and Merritt McKeon. *Stop Domestic Violence: An Action Plan for Saving Lives*. New York: St. Martin's Griffin, 1997.

Burgonio-Watson, Thelma. To Remember. Faith Trust Institute Newsletter, March 2005. Available from: http://www.faithtrustinstitute.org. Accessed February 20, 2006.

Cloud, Henry, and John Townsend. *Boundaries: When to Say Yes When to Say No to Take Control of Your Life*. Grand Rapids, MI: Zondervan, 1992.

Cone, James H. *For My People: Black Theology and the Black Church*. Maryknoll, NY: Orbis, 1984.

Cooper-White, Pamela. *The Cry of Tamar: Violence against Women and the Church's Response*. Minneapolis, MN: Fortress Press, 1995.

Creswell John W. *Research Design: Qualitative, Quantitative, and Mixed Methods Approaches*. Thousand Oaks, CA: Sage Publications, 2003.

Crittenden, E. Elaine Jack. "The Church and Domestic Violence." *The Christian Index* 139 (Sept. 2006): 30-32.

Diehl, Nancy J. *Sometimes...It is Sad to be at Home: What is a Kid to do about Domestic Violence?* Wayne County Michigan, Wayne County Council against Family Violence, 1997.

Esman, Abigail R. "If I Could Close My Eyes, A Story of Love, Pain, Hope, and Release." *Diane, The Curves Magazine* 3 (Fall 2006): 32-47.

Evans, Patricia. *The Verbally Abusive Relationship: How to Recognize It and How to Respond*. Holbrook, MA: Adams Media Corporation, 1996.

Fortune, Marie M. *Keeping the Faith, Guidance for Christian Women Facing Abuse*. San Francisco: Harper San Francisco, 1987.

_____. "Where are These Men? Part 2. "Faith Trust Institute Newsletter, 24 July 2007. Available from:

http://www.faithtrustinstitute.org., Accessed 25 July 2007.

George, William E. *The Book of Discipline of the Christian Methodist Episcopal Church 2006*. Memphis, TN: C.M.E. Publishing, 2006.

Haugen, David M. *Domestic Violence: Opposing Viewpoints*. Farmington Hill, MI: Greenhaven Press, 2005.

Herman, Judith, Trauma and Recovery: *The Aftermath of Violence – from Domestic Abuse to Political Terror*. New York: Basic Books, 1997.

Hertzberg, Hans W. *I and II Samuel: A Commentary*. London: SCM Press LTD, 1964.

Hutchinson, Susan. "I Finally Walked Out." *Medical Economics*, 5 August 2005, 66-67.

Jones, Ann. *Next Time, She'll Be Dead: Battering and How to Stop It*. Boston, MA: Beacon Press: Boston, MA, 1994.

Kammerer, Charlene, "Wednesday Worship Service-D.Min. Intensive." Lecture, United Theological Seminary, Trottwood, OH. 15 August 2007.

Kubany, Edward S., Mari A. McCaig, and Janet R. Laconsay. *Healing the Trauma of Domestic Violence: A Workbook for Women*. Oakland, CA: New Harbinger Publications, Inc., 2004.

Lindquest, Scott. *The Date Rape Prevention Book: The Essential Guide for Girls and Women*. Naperville, IL: Source Books, Inc., 2000.

Mbiti, John S. *African Religious and Philosophy*. Oxford: Heinermann, 1989.

McCarter, Jr., Kyle. Anchor Bible: *A New Translation with Introduction, Notes and Commentary of Second Samuel*. New York: Doubleday, 1984.

Miles, A. *Domestic Violence: What Every Pastor Needs to Know*. Minneapolis, MN: Augsburg Fortress Press, 2000.

_____. *Violence in Families: What Every Christian Needs to Know*. Minneapolis, MN: Augsburg Books, 2002.

Moser, Peter. *The History of Domestic Violence: Early Days of Domestic Violence, Police Intervention, Court Rulings*. Available from: http://abuse.sute101.com/article.cfm/the_history_of_domestic_violence. Accessed 10 October 2007.

Nason-Clark, Nancy and Catherine Clark Kroeger. *Refuge from Abuse: Healing and Hope for Abused Christian Women*. Downers Grove, IL: Inter Varsity Press, 2004.

_____. "When Terror Strikes at Home: The Interface Between Religion and Domestic Violence." *Journal for the Scientific Study of Religion* (2004): 303-310.

NiCarthy, Ginny. *Getting Free: A Handbook for Women in Abusive Relationships.* Seattle, WA: The Seal Press, 1982.

Park, Andrew Sung. *From Hurt to Healing: A theology of the Wounded.* Nashville, TN: Abindgon Press, 2004.

Reeves, Dianne. *In the Moment Live in Concert* (Capital Records, Inc. 4 July 2000). Roberts, Jeanne. *I Cry God! Hope and Healing for Survivors of Childhood Abuse.*
Oak Harbor, WA, Xlibris Press, 2003.

Sims, Jr. Theodore K. *Never Say Never: A Musical Gospel Stage Play* (Detroit, MI:
T & G Production, 2007). DVD.

Still, Susan. *Behind Closed Doors, Rarely Seen Domestic Violence.* Interview by Diane Sawyer, 20/20 Television Program, ABC-TV. 27 Oct 2006.

Trible, Phyllis, *Texts of Terror: Literary-Feminist Readings of Biblical Narratives.*
Philadelphia, PA: Fortress Press, 1984.

U.S. Department Health & Human Services, National Institute of Health. "Post- Traumatic Stress Disorder Research Fact Sheet." National Institute of Mental Health (NIMH) Homepage. Available from: http://www.nimh.nih.gov/health/publications/post-traumatic-stress-dis- order- research-fact-sheet.shtml. Accessed 30 July 2007.

Vann Antonia A. *Developing Culturally-Relevant Responses to Domestic Abuse: Asha Family Services, Inc.*

Harrisburg, PA: National Resources Center of Domestic Violence, 2003.

Wilson, Sandra D. *Hurt People Hurt People: When Your Pain Causes You to Hurt Those You Love*. Nashville, TN: Thomas Nelson Publishers, 1993.

Wimberly, Edward P. *Counseling African American Marriages and Families*.
Louisville, KY: Westminster John Knox Press, 1997.

Wolcott, Harry F. *Writing Up Qualitative Research*. Thousand Oaks, CA: Sage Publications, 1990.

CPSIA information can be obtained at www.ICGtesting.com
Printed in the USA
LVOW08s0206030315

428969LV00002B/86/P